From Blank Page to Bookshelf:
Your Guide to Self-Publishing
paperbacks and e-books

Tim Watkins

Waye Forward (Publishing) Ltd
Llanishen
Cardiff
CF14 5FA

ISBN-13: 978-0-9930877-2-1
ISBN-10: 0993087728

CONTENTS

Disclaimer

This work is based on the knowledge and experience gained from self-publishing using Amazon's CreateSpace and Kindle self-publishing platforms. It is in no way intended to give the impression that this book, its author or its author's companies are in anyway connected with those companies.

Nor should any of the services that the author and Waye Forward Ltd provide to other authors be in any way taken to be endorsed by or linked to CreateSpace or Kindle.

This book should be read only as a description of our experience as users/customers of these self-publishing platforms.

ABOUT THE AUTHOR

 Tim Watkins is a founder-director of Waye Forward Ltd, a company established to support those individuals and businesses that have previously been unable to access professional design and publishing services.

Tim Watkins graduated from a Russell Group University with a First Class economics degree in 1990.

Between 1990 and 1997 he worked as a policy researcher with the Welsh Consumer Council where he wrote and published several key policy reports including: *Quality of Life and Quality of Service* - an investigation into the provision of residential care homes for older people - and *In Deep Water* - an investigation into the many problems that followed the North Wales (Towyn) floods of February 1990.

Between 1998 and 2010, Tim Watkins was employed by the charity Depression Alliance Cymru, initially as a development worker, and between 2003 and 2010 as its Director. During that time he produced several mental health publications for the charity.

Between 2001 and 2010 Tim Watkins was appointed to sit on several Welsh Government advisory bodies including the *Health and Wellbeing Council for Wales*, the *Burrows-Greenwell Review of Mental Health Services in Wales* and the *Expert Panel on Depression.*

After 2010, Tim Watkins has authored a range of mental health-related books and booklets, together with two books about charities.

A qualified Life Coach, he also provides coaching, mentoring and support to other writers.

Introduction

Introduction

It has never been easier to publish and sell books than it is today. All of the objections and barriers that we have given as excuses for not writing have disappeared. A half-decent computer and an Internet connection are all you need to write, edit, typeset and self-publish your book in both print and e-book formats, and to find a truly global audience – meaning that you are guaranteed at least some sales.

The old adage that each of us has at least one book in us has never been truer than it is today. And who knows, you may turn out to be the next E.L. James (*50 Shades of Grey*) or J.K. Rowling (*Harry Potter*). There are plenty of people who claim to make a six-figure annual income from writing and selling Kindle e-books. But even if your goals are more modest – perhaps a few thousand pounds a year to pay for a holiday or toward a new car – today, writing and self-publishing books is an easy means of bringing in that additional income.

Sadly, though, most of us never get around to even thinking about writing a book, let alone seeing our work in print. There are many reasons. You may lack self-belief, thinking that books are only written by highly educated, professional experts. You may think that nobody will want to read what you have to say. You may believe that since you are highly unlikely to ever find a publisher, there is no point even starting to write. For many writers, technical barriers stand in the way. You may not be able to type. Or you may only be able to manage a couple of words a minute using two fingers. You may lack confidence using computer software to write, edit and typeset your work. And, again, if you believe that you are unlikely to find an audience or a publisher, you may never start to develop these skills.

These are the main reasons why most people never get around to writing and publishing their books… and they are based on a very old-fashioned view of publishing.

Modern computing and the Internet have changed everything. In the old days, it was hard to find a readership. You had no alternative than to get your book listed in publishers' catalogues and, hopefully, persuade bookshops and libraries to add your book to their shelves. Before you could get into print, you had to persuade a publishing company that your book was good enough to attract a large audience to buy enough of your books to recoup their investment and make a profit. Unfortunately, publishing houses were – and are – conservative institutions that want as close to guaranteed sales as they can get. This meant – and continues to mean – that new authors struggled to get a look in. With the old, hot metal printing presses book printing was an expensive, labour-intensive process. This meant that you needed to print at least 2,000 copies of a book to bring the unit cost down to a point where people would buy it. And, of course, in those days if you were lucky enough to get a publishing contract, you had to write your manuscript by hand, type it on a mechanical typewriter, or dictate it and pay someone to transcribe it.

When my first book was published in 1992, my only real input had been to write. An editor made the necessary amendments to my manuscript. Typesetting and cover design were carried out by a specialist at the printers. Proof reading was carried out by yet another editor. We printed two thousand copies; which we had to find storage space for. This all came at a huge cost – around £5,000 for the printing and a further £5,000 for the design and typesetting.

In those days, self-publishing was not really viable unless you had a lot of cash to throw around. Access to specialist book printing and binding technology was expensive. You could botch together a DIY publication using your home printer and a plastic ring-binder. But books and reports produced in this way looked shoddy and unprofessional.

In the mid-2000s things began to change. Several printing firms began to provide low-volume book printing services. At that time, I published several publications, printing just 500 copies per print run. By 2010, it was possible to produce as few as 50 books at a time. Unfortunately, even 50 books have to be stored somewhere. And if you have published several books, you can quickly use up your storage space.

Then there was the problem of selling books. Most of the books I wrote between 1990 and 2010 were published by organisations that were able to sell them through their mailing lists. They were also able to employ press and public relations professionals to get media coverage for the books – my 1992 book, *In Deep*

Water was covered by the main news channels in the UK on the day we published it. Selling your own book was much harder. Without an organisation behind you, it was much harder to get media attention. Bookshops were often reluctant to stock your book; and online stores like Amazon set design and stock criteria that made it difficult to get a book listed.

Until very recently, the only cost-effective option for most writers was the *blogsphere.* Open source web building platforms like WordPress allowed anyone with rudimentary IT skills to create a blog. In recent years blogs have proliferated and in some instances made their authors rich and famous. E-books seemed to be an extension of blogging, paving the way for independent writers to publish their work.

One of the myths of the 2000s was that e-books, blogs and websites would replace books, magazines and newspapers. Blog readers, however, turned out to be a very different audience. While electronic reading has undoubtedly dented print sales, the book market has stabilised. Millions of people continue to buy printed books, magazines and newspapers in preference to electronic versions of the same work. This said, as late as 2010, the publishing industry was still able to restrict the numbers of writers who could publish their work.

Between 2005 (in the USA) and 2013, everything changed. Amazon opened its' CreateSpace publishing platform to independent authors. This meant that any writer could self-publish their work and automatically sell it to a global readership via the Amazon website.

All that is required of you today is a bit of effort knuckling down and writing the book, together with some practice at using some very easy to use *and free* software. If you can use word-processing software there is nothing to prevent you from publishing and selling your book. The content and cover templates provided by Amazon will suffice to produce a professional looking, self-published book. Or, with a bit of effort and the use of some free design and typesetting software, it is entirely possible for you to create a professional design of your own.

The Self-Publishing Revolution

The Self-Publishing Revolution

The written word has always been bound up with power and authority. When archaeologists unearthed the first clay tablets, they found not poetry or prayer, but inventory – information about harvests and the re-distribution of resources to soldiers and to the labourers who worked the fields. Only the literate minority could control this crucial information, and through it, the population as a whole. More recently, the Catholic Church used the Latin language to deny people access to the religious texts that formed the ruling ideology of medieval Europe. This is why the development of the printing press and the publication of the Gutenberg Bible were so revolutionary.

The invention of the printing press and the theft from the Chinese of the formula for making cheap paper paved the way for the European Enlightenment. This, in turn, paved the way for the revolutions of the eighteenth century. The freedom to write and publish pamphlets, newspapers and books was seen as so important to the emerging democracies that the "right to a free press" was enshrined in the American constitution.

In the post-war years, printing was labour-intensive. Print workers' skills were exclusive, so the print unions were able to (temporarily) block change and maintain high wages. This had a knock-on effect on the structure of publishing. Setting up a book for printing incurred the bulk of the production costs. Once these costs had been incurred, there was little additional cost in increasing the number of books printed. The greater the sales, the more profitable a book could be. A minimum print run spread the set up costs so that the cover price would be affordable.

Some specialist publishers did produce non-fiction books for particular audiences. Smaller print runs meant higher book prices. Publishers were limited to subject areas (such as university courses) where relatively high sales could be achieved. For the most part though, publishers sought books to sell at a low price to a mass audience. And since publishers have tended to be risk-averse, this has meant sticking with existing authors rather than risking losing money with new and unknown authors while avoiding niche subject areas where traditional approaches would lose money.

So traditional publishing has been elitist. Its approach had been further bolstered by the high costs of marketing and distribution. Even if an independent author could get a book printed, they would struggle to get anyone to notice, and would be unlikely to get their book onto the shelves of leading bookshops.

In 1995 the supermarkets rejected the longstanding Net Book Agreement which maintained artificially high book prices. As a result, the market became even more cut-throat. The majority of book sales were now in outlets like Asda and Tesco rather than traditional bookshops. Prices were low, so only best selling authors were worth investing in. New authors experienced even greater difficulty attracting a publisher. Even previously published mid-ranking authors were struggling to get their books published.

But the foundations of a digital publishing revolution were also in place by the early-2000s.

In 2007 Amazon released the first Kindle e-reader. The Kindle proved attractive to book readers. The link with Amazon's book distribution platform, attracted budding authors who could for the first time reach a mass audience.

Today e-books are an accepted part of the publishing landscape. Those within the publishing industry who claimed that e-books would never take off were wrong. But those who claimed that e-books would replace printed books have also been proved wrong. In the USA in 2013, half of the population owned an e-book reader, and 28 percent had read at least one e-book during the year. However, 69 percent of Americans had read at least one printed book during the year as well. And both figures were up on previous years.

The markets for e-books and print books are vibrant. But until now, e-books have been the only commercial option available to authors who are unable secure a contract with a publishing company. But Amazon will change all this.

A few years ago, developments in print technology made it economical to print books one at a time. Internet-based platforms such as Lulu began offering authors the opportunity to make their books available on a print-on-demand basis. Crucially, there was no up-front cost to authors. However Lulu lacked the mass audience to make print-on-demand books widely available. And this often meant that authors could not sell sufficient books to make an income from them.

In 2005, Amazon had taken over two companies – Book Surge and Custom Flix – and repackaged them as "CreateSpace". Initially, CreateSpace operated in the USA, producing print-on-demand books, CDs and DVDs. However, the CreateSpace platform was opened up to UK authors in 2013 and to European authors in 2014. Both the CreateSpace and Kindle platforms allow authors to upload books in common formats such as Microsoft .doc and Adobe .pdf. This means that even the least computer literate authors can access the platforms to get their work published – although in practice, the more work that goes into the design and layout of a book, the greater the chance of selling it. From Amazon's perspective, the more authors and books they can get onto their publishing platforms, the more sales they can make. For this reason, they offer particularly generous royalty rates to authors – particularly those authors who agree to publish exclusively with them. These authors receive a royalty rate of 70 percent (compared to 35 percent for those who also publish on other sites). Contrast this with the 20 percent or so that an author receives from a traditional publishing house. Moreover, Amazon pay royalties monthly compared to most publishing houses that pay 6-monthly or even annually. Amazon Royalties are paid 6-weeks in arrears, but payments are monthly after the first payment.

These technical advances are "revolutionary" in a sense. However, this is not why I refer to this as a publishing revolution. The real revolution is not the technology itself, but what it allows people to do. It is important to understand the power of both e-books and print-on-demand books *when coupled to* a mass sales platform with a global customer base.

Imagine that you had a wealth of knowledge about a subject so narrow that only a few local people were likely to be interested in. A traditional publisher simply would not be interested in anything you wrote, because it would be impossible to reach enough of your potential audience to make it worthwhile. So, until recently, your only option would be to print your book yourself, and hope to sell enough copies to recoup the cost (or simply accept the loss). But today you can write, design and publish a book at no (financial) cost. You can make it available to a worldwide audience. Where you would have struggled to sell 20 books locally, you can sell hundreds or even thousands of copies worldwide.

This access to minority audiences in niche subjects is the real revolution in publishing that we are living through today. Because it is now possible to write a book on just about any topic you can think of and reach an audience who are interested in it. Today, the idea that we all have at least one book in us is no longer a throw-away line. It is now an opportunity for you not only to write your book, but to sell it to an audience that is interested enough to pay for it.

In the rest of this book I will take you, step-by-step through the process of writing, editing, designing and typesetting, coding (for e-books), publishing and marketing your book.

Tools of the Trade

Tools of the Trade

Contemporary self-publishing involves the creation of digital information that can be converted into two key end products – print-on-demand paperback books and electronic books. This means that you have to be able to gather your thoughts and ideas and get them down on (electronic) paper.

You will need a reasonably good Internet-connected PC, Laptop, Notebook or Tablet that can run word processing software. These do not need to be top-of-the-range. Indeed, a reasonably-priced, basic model will suffice. Nor do you need to pay a lot of money for word processing software. Free open source software such as *Open Office* or *Google Docs* is all you really need to create the manuscript for your book.

It is also worth carrying a real paper notebook and pens with you for times when you do not have access to a computer. While you won't want to write volumes of text in this format, it is a handy way of jotting down ideas that you might otherwise forget by the time you sit down at your computer.

A Dictaphone provides an alternative to pen and paper. These can be stand-alone recorders that will create an audio recording that you will have to transcribe later on. However, several Dictaphones have been designed to operate alongside the *Dragon Naturally Speaking* "speech-to-text" software, which will automatically translate your spoken words into word processed text.

Most of us write (or dictate) into a word processing programme. New computers come with at least one word processing programme pre-installed. For example, computers running the Windows operating system have a programme called *Word Pad*, which is sufficient to write a book. However, some writers prefer more versatile software such as *MS Word*, as these tend to be better for printing out readable drafts of a manuscript on a home printer. Others opt for software designed by authors with authors in mind. For example, *Scrivener* is much more than a word processor, allowing research materials and sources to be opened and read within the programme, and allowing paragraphs and chapters to be edited and re-ordered without compromising the whole book.

The research capabilities of *Scrivener* can also be found in the open source *Zotero* software often used by academic researchers to create mini reference libraries for each of their projects. *Zotero* integrates with most web browsers, so that you can save a snapshot of any web page you want to reference in your text. It will also store online .pdf files so that you can easily find them in future. *Zotero* also integrates with word processing software such as MS Word, allowing you to easily reference any of the research papers that you include in your finished book.

While *Scrivener* and *Zotero* can make life easier, in practice a computer and some word processing software are the only tools you need to write, edit and publish your book. The cloud-based software used by Amazon's self-publishing platforms will convert your document into both print and e-book formats. They will also give you free access to their cover design software, and more than 900 royalty-free images that can be incorporated into the final design of your book cover. However, you need to put some effort into creating your book, so that it will stand out from the crowd when you come to publish it.

While you could publish your word processed manuscript direct into print, this will limit what you can do to optimise the look and feel of your final book. Common limitations are:

○ Choice of fonts is limited
○ It is difficult to set up and change paragraph styles
○ You cannot control margins, headers and footers
○ You cannot insert or properly place images into your text.

While relatively expensive software, such as *Microsoft Word*, will allow this to some extent, even these programmes can cause headaches when you try to convert your manuscript into a print-ready file using the software on Amazon's platforms. The problem here is that while most word process software has been built to give you a "what-you-see-is-what-you-get" (WYSIWYG) interface for printing to a home printer, it achieves this by inserting lots of different software commands behind the scenes. When you come to convert your document, the conversion software is confused by these commands, leading to errors with the layout of the final book. For example, paragraphs may not flow properly; margins may shift position; bullet lists may not work; and font sizes may change. It can take days for you to figure out what is causing the problem, and how to put it right.

It is important to remember that the sole purpose of the word processing software you choose is to get your ideas down on paper. At this stage you should not be concerned with the layout and design of your final book. Indeed, even copy editing issues (spelling, grammar, pace, etc) can, within reason, be left for later. In publishing, a first draft is often referred to as a SFD ("shitty first draft") precisely because it is expected to contain mistakes and styling problems that need to be dealt with in the editing process.

Once you have completed your first draft, you will need editing software to highlight potential problems. Most editing software is "cloud-based". That is, you have to upload your text to an Internet-based platform that will use algorithms to pick up potential problems. There are some free platforms, like *ProWritingAid*, which will check for potential problems such as over-used words, clichés, pacing and writing style, as well as standard spelling and grammar issues. If you are prepared to pay, you could try the *AutoCrit* platform. However, because this platform charges a monthly fee, it can quickly become expensive. *AutoCrit* is of more value to professional editors who make a living from editing work for lots of authors than for an individual author who produces just two or three books a year.

While the reliability of editing algorithms is likely to improve over time, these editing platforms are in their infancy. It would be a mistake to rely on them alone. You will want another human to look through your manuscript once you have made your own edits. You can find professional copy editors via an Internet search. Charges will vary according to the type of edit you require. A basic edit is unlikely to cost too much. However, this will involve a single individual reading through your manuscript and marking up potential problems, so there remains scope for error. A more comprehensive edit of your copy will involve at least two people reading your text (including punctuation) out loud in order to pick up errors and issues. This process will lead to a much better final manuscript, but is likely to cost considerably more.

In the end, "you pay your money and you take your choice!" But remember, readers' experiences and the ratings and reviews they give will determine how well your final book sells. While most readers will forgive the odd spelling mistake, they are unlikely to accept a book that is riddled with mistakes and grammatical errors.

Once the editing process is complete and you have made the necessary changes to your work, you will have your final word processed document. You could publish at this point. However, you will most probably find that your word processing software is incompatible to some extent with the Amazon CreateSpace platform. The result is that the "proof" (a document showing how your book will look in print) of your book will appear differently to how you intended. In any case, you will need to ensure that the document you upload to the CreateSpace platform is an accepted book size. Since most word processing software uses a sheet of A4 paper (the standard size for home printers) as the default, you will have to change the setup of your file. And while you could use one of the .doc templates provided by CreateSpace, you will most probably find that this ends up looking very different in your print proof from how it appeared on your computer screen – and this can take days to sort out.

I recommend using desktop publishing (DTP) software to work on the layout of the print version of your final book. If you have *Microsoft Office* installed, then you could use *MS Publisher* to typeset your book. I have done this in the past. However, I found that *Publisher* does not do all the tasks I want. I also found various niggling faults with the software, including problems with handling images. If you have enough money, you could obtain a copy of *Adobe In-Design*. This is the software of choice in the design and publishing industry. But at more than £300 for a single user license, this is a very expensive option. Fortunately, there are several cheaper DTP packages that will do 95 percent of what *In-Design* will do at a fraction of the price. My own favourite is Serif's *PagePlus* software (used to typeset this book). Serif has a free demo version of the software which is sufficient for typesetting a book. However, many of the features found in the full version of this software are not available in the free version, so you may want to upgrade. A good free alternative is *Scribus*, an open source DTP package. This software will also allow you to typeset your book. I have used *Scribus* to produce magazines and brochures, and would recommend it to anyone who is operating on a budget. However, it is not as easy to use as some of the paid DTP software.

Whatever software you are drawn to, it is essential that it allows you to export your final book as a print-ready .pdf file. Using this output format (unlike word processing files) will mean that your book will appear in print exactly as you intended it to. Indeed, the CreateSpace platform converts other formats into print ready .pdfs prior to printing. And it is this conversion process that results in many of the layout problems that people who use word processed documents experience. By creating your own .pdf file, to all extents and purposes you by-pass the file conversion process.

Hidden word processing software commands embedded in your manuscript are an even bigger problem when you come to creating an e-book. This is because e-books are very different from printed books.

In print, I can decide what fonts to use, what type sizes, line spacing, margins, headers and footers, etc. These are all fixed in the print-ready .pdf document that I upload for publishing. The CreateSpace publishing platform simply prints each book to my specifications.

With e-books the situation is reversed. It does not matter what typesetting I prefer; with e-books, the reader makes all the choices. Each Kindle device can be set up to display text as the user chooses. And if I try to specify text settings, these may well conflict, causing errors in the book layout. You could take a gamble on this, and simply convert your print-ready file and hope things do not go wrong. But remember that a bad reading experience will result in bad reviews and ratings. Having worked hard writing your book, why spoil it for want of an extra day making it ready as an e-book?

The only reliable way to create great e-books is to encode them in the same way a web developer codes a website. An e-book is best thought of as a single basic web page set up to appear on a Kindle device rather than an Internet browser. This is the main reason why the e-books created by commercial publishing houses are so much more expensive than those created by amateurs is that it takes knowledge and time to code them. And the publishing houses want you to pay for the time they put in.

If you are committed enough to write a book, you are more than intelligent enough to learn some basic HTML (structure) and CSS (styling) codes to make your book display properly on any e-reader. And there is plenty of help here (and online) if you are prepared to take some time to learn. When you are ready to code your e-book, you will need a basic html editor. I have recently begun to use *Adobe Brackets* an open source code editor that works in conjunction with the *Google Chrome* browser so that you can watch the changes you make to your book in real time. Alternatively, if all else fails, the simple *Notepad* application that comes with any Microsoft Windows operating system can double as a simple code editor.

Amazon's Kindle platform contains some book templates that you can use as a starting point for coding your book. Indeed, you could simply cut and paste your work into a template and then save it for publication. The aim is to create a folder containing your coded content (this will be an html file similar to a website), any separate style sheets that you create, and any images used in your book.

In order to publish your coded e-book to the Kindle platform, you will either need to download a small piece of software called *KindleGen* provided by Amazon, or you will need to find some third-party conversion software. Although Amazon recommends *KindleGen*, it means that you need to code several additional files to complete your e-book, whereas third-party conversion software will generate these automatically. I have used a free conversion programme called *Calibre 64 bit*. This software will take your html file (together with any images that appear in the book) and packages them into a range of different e-book formats, including the .mobi files required for Kindle. Some DTP software and several cloud-based platforms claim to be able to convert a publication into an e-book format. Because these are in their infancy, they should be treated with caution. If you do choose to create an e-book in this way, you should check your book thoroughly using Amazon's *Kindle Previewer* software to ensure that it appears correctly on all types of Kindle devices.

You will need the *Kindle Previewer* software from Amazon to review your e-book before uploading it to the Kindle platform. This is essential because e-book reading devices are considerably less versatile than web browsers, so you need to check that any style elements you included in your book file will actually display properly on the full range of Kindle devices.

Finally, you will need to create a cover for your book. Remember that your cover is the main thing that potential readers are going to see when they come across your book on Amazon. So taking time and effort on a cover that stands out is an essential investment.

Both CreateSpace and Kindle platforms contain a free Cover Creator that allows you to choose from a range of templates and nearly 1,000 royalty-free images. These can be combined to produce attractive cover designs that will highlight your book to potential readers. The risk here is that potential readers may see that the cover is a common template, and this may deter them from purchasing your book. The more adventurous and creative among us can create and upload their own cover design either as an image or a print-ready .pdf file. This allows for a book cover that is unique, and that will stand out from the crowd. The desktop publishing software used to create the content of the book can also be used to create a cover[*]. It is simply a matter of creating the artwork and artistic fonts that you want to use.

---

[*] CreateSpace provide .pdf templates for the dimensions of book covers but you will have to calculate the spine width based on the number of pages.

Alternatively, you can create your cover in image editing software such as *Adobe Photoshop*. As with DTP software, there are several less expensive photo imaging packages – such as Serif's *PhotoPlus* –that will do 95 percent of what *Photoshop* can do. And if you are working on a budget, there is an open source package called *GIMP* that is reasonably versatile.

These are all the tools you need to write your book and create a professional end product. It is possible, then, to go from blank page to published book and e-book using open source (free) software. Of course, you may prefer to pay for the additional features offered by other software packages. And if you have the resources, you may even want to invest in the industry standard *Adobe Creative Suite* – although at more than £2,000 per licence, this is really only worthwhile for major publishers.

Read Before You Write

Read Before You Write

I may seem to be stating the blindingly obvious when I say "read before you write". But I am not just talking about the need to carefully research your subject before writing it up (in the way that all good research students are taught). Even if you are writing non-fiction, as well as knowing your subject, expression is vital. I advise you to look at how other writers present their work. What language style do they use? What persona do they adopt? Are they easy to read? And if not, can you see why not?

Academic writers are notorious for papers and books designed to obscure their subject and exclude all but the most determined reader. These writers had fallen into academic "dialects" – ways of speaking that are understood by academic insiders, but which serve to confuse the outsider. The justification for this kind of writing is to present complex ideas in shorthand form to an audience of insiders who already understand them. These writers all too often presented papers and books for public consumption using the same dialects.

If your aim is to make your book widely available, then you need to do the exact opposite. You need to present your writing in a form that is easily accessible to your audience. However, one can go too far in this direction too. There are writers who write as if their audience were children. And while this can guarantee that ideas are broken down into easily understandable chunks, and presented in very plain language, it all too often appears patronising. It reads as if the writer thinks the reader is an idiot.

One essential option is to explore style guides of organisations that publish lots of authors. For example, Wikipedia has its own house style guide on its website. Most newspapers have similar style guides, as do broadcasters and government departments. You can also find guides of book publishing houses. These style guides set out how they expect their authors to write, and include everything from reading age to punctuation and from paragraph length to referencing. These guides are invaluable for helping you develop grammar, spelling and punctuation. However, they are seldom enough to help you develop your own personal writing style. For this, you must read widely.

As we read, we become familiar with the ways different authors present their ideas. For the most part, we unconsciously decide whether we like a particular author. There is just something about their clarity, pace, style and language use that enables an easy read. When we encounter such writers, we can re-read their work with a view to analysing what it is about it that makes it such an easy read. One reason to do this – and a good approach to writing – is plainly and simply to "steal" it! I don't mean imitate, or incorporate. I mean, adopt the writing style and use it in your own writing. Obviously, I am talking about the writing style at this point; I am not suggesting that you plagiarise other people's work, infringe copyright or reproduce passages without crediting the author.

In many creative disciplines, there is a saying that "rules are there to be broken… but only when you understand why the rules are there." Only when you have understood what is good about other writing styles will you fully develop a writing style of your own. With practice, you begin to understand how each writing style works. And as you start to understand a whole range of styles, so you will find yourself interchanging and building on them until, ultimately, you develop your own personal style. In this sense, learning to write is similar to learning art or music. Artists often begin by imitating other artists. So do musicians. This is not just about the great artists, musicians and writers, but about anyone whose style catches your attention. Over time, imitation and innovation come together to allow each artist, musician and writer to develop their own unique style.

Writing Your Book - Fiction

Writing Your Book - Fiction

There is no one best way to write your book. A good writer will take considerable care in helping readers to suspend their disbelief – the disbelief that is, to forget that they are reading a book, and instead believe that they are listening to a true story. To achieve this, it is essential that the "facts" within your story do not jar with your readers. For example, if you set your book in any historical period, you will need to describe accurately the background to that period. It is essential that you do not introduce the kind of mistakes seen in some Hollywood movies, such as where the Roman gladiator wears a wrist watch! If you are writing about the year 1900, you need to be sure that everything – including the characters – is accurate for that time. If you do not, I can guarantee that some readers will make a point of letting you know... at worst, by giving your book negative reviews.

Understanding and mapping out the structure of your book are essential first steps to writing. You may choose to use specialist software like the *Scrivener* package to develop the various elements of your book's structure. Since the software was designed by an author for other authors, it allows you to develop and properly file the various elements. However, you can use simple word processing software or even pen and paper (and a well-organised file) just to develop each of the elements. Here are eight essential elements within the structure of your book that you will need to develop:

○ Theme
○ Plot

- Time
- Place
- Narration
- Characters
- Opening
- Ending.

The theme of your book concerns the ideas that lie beneath the story. Your book may, in essence be about big human issues such as love, deceit, jealousy, compassion, hate, death, etc. You will need to think about how you are going to present this underlying theme by considering how you want your readers to respond. For example, you might want your readers to think deeply about the issues raised. Alternatively, you might want to present a serious issue in a light-hearted manner so that your readers feel entertained and amused alongside being introduced to profound ideas.

Your plot is the story (or stories) that run through your book from start to finish. This involves thinking through questions such as:

- What happens?
- When?
- Who is present?
- What motivates them?

Most writers take time and care to map out their story from start to finish, plotting when various characters and events occur, and how these impact on the rest of the story. Again, it can be useful to quite literally draw a map or plan, either using software or a pen and paper.

It is useful to work out the time scale of your story. In part, this means deciding whether your story is condensed into a single day, or whether it extends over weeks, months or years. In part it is also about deciding how you will tell the story. For example, you might simply tell the story in chronological order; describing the events as they occur in time. However, you could use devices such as flashbacks to allow your story to move backward and forward in time.

Deciding about the place or places where your story occurs is about both space and time. That is, it covers both the geographical location(s) *and* the historical period(s). In some cases, these details will be essential to the development of the story, and will need to be developed in order to lead your readers to the conclusion of your book.

Narration is about how your story is told; and by whom. Your narrator can take the role of an all-seeing third party who is telling the story as it unfolds. Alternatively, your narrator might be one of the characters who is telling the story from their point of view. This approach can be developed so that a story has several narrators, each telling the story from their own viewpoint in order to build a bigger picture. Using a character or characters as your narrator also allows you add interest by creating a situation in which your readers know *or think they know* more than the narrator.

The characters in your book must be credible and consistent if your story is to work. The last think you want is to unintentionally have one or more of your characters undergo personality transplants or physical transformations as your story unfolds. Readers will have difficulty continuing to believe your story if a character suddenly acts *out of character*.

The best way of guarding against this is to write up a separate character profile for each of your characters. This profile should include:

○ Every aspect of their physical appearance

○ Their personal history

○ Their personality traits and habits.

You should also consider how you want your readers to feel about each character. Should the reader like, love, mistrust or hate them? Whatever they feel about them, they still must be sufficiently convincing that your readers will be fascinated by them.

Obviously, you will need to spend more time developing these profiles for your main characters than you will for a character that appears just once in the story. Nevertheless, it is worth developing the background for your characters to the point that you can believe in them, as this will help you to convince your readers too.

Getting the opening of your book right is essential. Your opening is like the headline on the front page of a newspaper – it is what grabs the readers' attention and creates sufficient interest that they want to read the rest of the story. With self-publishing, the opening is especially important because the Amazon platform displays the beginning of almost all of the books on display, both print and e-books. It is the opening that will persuade readers to buy, so it has to create the intrigue, excitement and interest to cause your readers to want to know more.

Finally, think about how you want your readers to feel at the when they come to the end of your story. The way your ending is written will determine this. Unless you intend writing a series, your ending should bring all of the threads of the story together. You will need to decide whether your ending will be inevitable or whether it will close with an unexpected twist.

Mapping out your book in this way will help you to keep to the story, and avoid the temptation of rambling off into irrelevant asides. It will help you maintain the authenticity of your story and the credibility of your characters. However, while it can guide you and help you to structure your book, only you can actually *write* the story.

Writing Your Book - Non-Fiction

Writing Your Book - Non-Fiction

Much non-fiction writing is formulaic. Nevertheless, it still tells a story. If you are writing non-fiction it is essential to map out the structure of your book, and to decide exactly what you want your readers to take away from it. You may also want to consider elements such as the style that you use to present your ideas. Are you presenting your work in a matter of fact manner (as you would in an academic journal) or do you want it to be more dramatic (as you would for a magazine article)?

Standard academic writing often follows the structure used by most journals:

○ Introduction
○ Methods
○ Results
○ Discussion
○ Conclusion.

The *Introduction* will explain the question(s) that the book seeks to answer. It will also explain why these are important issues, and indicate research and discussions that have already taken place.

The *Methods* used in any research carried out for the book are an essential part of any academic work, as they allow your readers to decide how reliable your results are. There is a hierarchy of evidence, with the opinions of experts at the bottom, questionnaire surveys in the middle, and randomised, controlled, double-blinded trials at the top. You should explain why you chose a particular method, and what its strengths and weaknesses are. Readers need to know this in order to judge your results.

The way you set out your *Results* will depend upon the methods used. If you have conducted a trial or a survey, you will present statistical data that may require tables or charts to help readers absorb the information. If, on the other hand, you have conducted qualitative research or are presenting secondary data, you may need to quote your sources within your narrative.

Your *Discussion* should help readers understand your work within the context of the wider discussion referred to in the introduction. Are the results in line with previous research? Or does the research contradict previous studies? What new information or ideas do you bring to the discussion?

The *Conclusion* is what readers will take away from your work. In concluding, you may want to refer back to the question you set out to answer, before summarising your results and how these affect the wider debate.

An alternative form of non-fiction writing uses a dialectical approach:

○ Thesis
○ Antithesis
○ Synthesis.

This approach is more useful where you are drawing on other people's work to tell your "story"; essentially setting out what you think about what other people have said about a topic. You set out your basic argument (thesis). You then explain to the readers how this argument has been challenged and criticised (antithesis). Finally, you pull the salient points and issues from both to form a wider and more coherent picture (synthesis).

This approach can be particularly useful when writing about large-scale issues where different writers have arrived at various conclusions based on the same source data. For example, if you were writing about climate change or global economics, you will find a large number of writers who share the same basic data, but disagree vigorously about what the data mean.

By presenting all sides of the argument, about a difficult subject, your book can speak authoritatively to your readers, leading them to the conclusion that you want them to take away.

Getting Started

Getting Started

There comes a time when you have to stop thinking *about* your book, and actually sit down and write it. Once you have all of your background materials and data together, and you have mapped out your book, all that is left is to *start writing*!

I cannot emphasise this enough – your intention is to develop a very rough version first. It doesn't matter if you make mistakes or grammatical errors, these will be dealt with during the editing process. Nor do you need to spend time thinking about presentation; this will be dealt with during typesetting and cover design. The task in hand is solely to *write*!

The secret to getting started is to *get started*. It may sound obvious, but what I mean is that most writers (myself included) spend far too much time thinking and far too little time knuckling down to the process of getting words down on paper. This is procrastination and it is the curse of many creative people.

All too often, creative people will distract ourselves rather than make a start on our creative work. Why should this be? There are several reasons; most commonly:

○ Perfectionism
○ Too wide a topic
○ Inadequate background research
○ Poor time management.

It is worth remembering that the first job in the process of writing your book is to create a rough draft. Nobody creates a perfect book to begin with. Nor would anyone who knows about publishing expect you to. As we will see later, all manuscripts require several edits before they are ready to be typeset and printed. So rather than worrying that your work may not be perfect, just focus on getting your ideas out of your mind and onto the page – we can come back and correct mistakes, or even re-write whole chapters later on.

It is well worth keeping to the old 80 percent/20 percent rule. This says that it takes just 20 percent of your time and energy to create something that achieves 80 percent of its purpose; i.e. it is "good enough". On the other hand, it will take the remaining 80 percent of your time and energy trying to achieve the remaining 20 percent of your purpose. And nobody has ever written a 100 percent perfect book!

You should also consider "chunking", especially when writing non-fiction. This is because when your subject is too wide, it can be difficult to know where to start. For example, if you had to write a book about "the economy" where would you start? But if, on the other hand, you had only to write about "the £1 coin", you could easily write about:

○ The history of the pound
○ The transition from notes to coins
○ The process of minting the coins
○ The metals they are made from
○ The various pictures and inscriptions that are used.

Of course, if you have not done your research – or if you have forgotten your sources – you can end up staring into space simply because you lack the knowledge and information to write authoritatively. Research is too wide a topic to cover here. However, at the very least, you need to have copies of any books or articles that you intend drawing on together with Internet links to any online research materials immediately to hand while you are writing. The *Scrivener* and *Zotero* software can be very useful for keeping your research materials in one, easily accessible place. However, at the very least you should set up a file structure on your computer, and/or a ring binder and written notes, so that you can save all your reference materials into a single folder.

Some of us also struggle with time management. One way around this is to work to deadlines, as these create a sense of urgency that encourages us to work harder and faster. Although this can be difficult when you are working for yourself, one option is to use a timer or an alarm clock to create a deadline to finish a section or a chapter. For example, you might give yourself an hour to complete a chapter. To reinforce this, you might create a reward (for example, a cup of coffee, a bar of chocolate or a glass of wine) for when you succeed.

This leads to another consideration – the speed at which you can get your ideas written down. There are several free online tools that you can use to check your typing speed. The average typing speed is 46 words per minute. A good professional typist will manage more than 75 words per minute. And while you do not need to be as fast as a professional, if your typing speed is less than average, you will need a lot more time to finish your book.

Dictation is the only viable alternative to typing. Here you have two choices. First, you can record an audio file then pay a transcription service to type it for you. Rates for this vary, and are usually based on the number of minutes of audio recording you want transcribed, the quality of the recording, and the turnaround time. This is unlikely to offer value for money to someone who does not have the luxury of an advance (payment) from a publishing company. Your second option is to use speech recognition software which automatically converts your spoken words into written text. Free speech recognition software is available, but is currently too inaccurate to use for book writing. At the time of writing, Nuance's *Dragon Naturally Speaking* is the only speech recognition software on the market that is accurate enough to allow you to begin writing immediately. Moreover, because it learns from its mistakes, the more you use this software the greater its accuracy becomes.

A final consideration concerns the environment in which you will write. Clearly, if you intend dictating your book, you will need somewhere quiet and secluded. However, in the end the choice of environment will vary from author to author. Whereas some of us need a dedicated writing space, others are able to write on the move – for example, writing sections of their book while commuting by train or while taking a break in a café. Only you can figure out what kind of environment you need to work in.

Just do not let noise and disturbance become an excuse for not getting started.

Editing

Editing

An important rule when writing your manuscript is to save the edits for later. While it is fine to attend to spelling mistakes and obvious grammatical errors, anything more than this can wait until the first draft of your manuscript is complete.

Most word processing software that comes with spelling and grammar checking, and these can be helpful; just don't rely on them. Here are just a few common writing mistakes that spell-checkers will miss:

- To/two/too - easy to misuse these when you are writing in a hurry
- They're/their/there
- Whose/who's
- You're/your
- Its/it's
- Angel/angle
- In/ion – the letters "I" and "o" are next to each other on a keyboard so it is easy to hit both together... and "in" is a very common word
- Sing/sign
- Meat/meant
- Moth/month
- Word/world.

To begin with, you will probably need to go through your manuscript several times, attending to spelling mistakes, grammatical errors, omissions and misplaced chapters, sections and paragraphs. However, reading your own work over and over results in a word blindness in which errors that would be obvious to a new reader fail to enter your consciousness. In part, this is because when you read a word over and over, it loses its meaning. In part it is because when you read your own words and you know what they are supposed to say, your unconscious mind will fill in any gaps or cover over any mistakes. There is simply no way that any author – no matter how good they are – can be relied on to edit their own work. Nor is there a publishing house that would send a book to print without having edited it independently (often several times over).

It is essential that once you have made all the obvious amendments to your manuscript, you hand it over to a fresh reader (hopefully somebody with a good grasp of language and grammar) to carry out an additional edit of your manuscript.

This independent editing is often (wrongly) referred to as "proof reading". In fact, the term "proof reading" dates from the days before digital printing. Because print costs were high, a proof copy of a book would be printed and checked thoroughly for any errors both of language and layout before final approval was given to go ahead with printing. Nowadays, what we refer to as proof reading is more correctly what was known as copy-editing. There are broadly three types of copy-editing:

○ The use of built-in spell checking and grammar checking within word processor software (as we have seen, this is very inadequate and should not be relied on)

- ○ A visual read-through, marking up any changes you wish to make (this is a more thorough process, but should still not be relied on)
- ○ A complete audio read-through (i.e. reading aloud) in which one person reads while another marks up errors in the manuscript.

At the very least you should ask an independent reader to carry out a visual read-through. And ideally, you should ask them to carry out an audio read-through in order to optimise the edit.

Done properly, editing is a highly skilled and labour-intensive process. For this reason, you may wish to pay an editor to go through your work in detail. After all, having put a great deal of effort into writing your book, it would be a shame to spoil it for want of paying a few pounds that you will most likely recoup in royalties within a few weeks of publishing it.

Typesetting

Typesetting

You have written your manuscript; edited it several times yourself; and had at least one independent person check through it too. Now it is time to think about the look and feel of your final book.

It is important to exercise caution at this point. You should only begin working on typesetting your book when you are sure that all necessary editorial changes have been made. Otherwise, you risk putting a lot of work into the layout of your book, only to see it all messed up when you have to make even minor editorial changes.

In theory, it is possible to typeset your book using your word processing software. Indeed, the CreateSpace publishing platform provides .doc templates for all the standard book publishing sizes. However, there are risks. As we have seen, with word processing what you see is not always what you get. Lines and paragraphs that appear to hang together on screen turn out not to do so in the final print proof. This can cause major headaches as you try to sort out what has gone wrong. To avoid these problems I recommend typesetting your book using a desktop publishing package.

The look and feel of your book start with the book size you choose. Since most of the content of your book will be text, black and white printing is the best option. Colour printing is far expensive than black and white, and will eat into your royalties. So unless your book depends on colour images, it is best to work in black and white. The size of your book will also help to determine its cost, and the royalties you will receive.

For example, the most common book size used in the publishing industry is 6 inches (15.24 cm) by 9 inches (22.86 cm). Using this size will optimise your income from royalties.

Having chosen the size of your book, you need to begin by thinking about how you want it to look and feel. While much of this is a matter of personal taste, you should always bear in mind that you want your readers to enjoy reading your book. This will depend on factors such as your margin sizes, line height, text size and fonts.

Much of the language of typesetting relates to old fashioned printing processes that involved hammering letter blocks into a print frame on giant rollers which would then press the inked letters onto paper as it rolled through the printing press. This is a subject in itself, and not one that we have space to cover here. However, it is worth understanding some typesetting issues.

Perhaps the most important is the difference between serif and sans serif fonts. The word "serif" refers to the small embellishments added to the letters in some font faces; the Times New Roman font is a common example. In theory, serif fonts make it easier to read large blocks of text. Sans serif simply means without serifs; the **Arial** font is a common example. Sans serif fonts make it easier to read small amounts of text such as that used on signs and fliers.

You may decide to choose one font for the body of your work, and a different -- perhaps more artistic -- font for chapter headings and other headings throughout the book. It is never a good idea to use an artistic font (𝖑𝖎𝖐𝖊 𝖙𝖍𝖎𝖘 𝖔𝖓𝖊) for the body of your book. Consistency is the key; once you have chosen a font you should use it throughout.

In addition to the font(s) that you choose, you will also need to think about the size of the type face. Choose one too small and people will struggle to read the book. Go for too large a type face and it will appear poorly designed. In most cases a 10 to 12 point font will usually work. However, you should be aware that the "point size" of a font refers not to the typeface itself, but to the block on which the letters were originally carved for use on an old fashioned printing press. As a result of different fonts can look much bigger or much smaller despite being the same point size:

THESE are each **different** twelve POINT fonts!

In the end, the choice of font and of type size is a matter of common sense. Put yourself in the readers' shoes, and ask whether your choice is likely to be comfortable and attractive.

Having chosen font and type size, you need to think about the margins and line spacing that you will use throughout the book. Common sense will help you again here – put yourself in your readers' place. Obviously, if the margins are too narrow then your text will run into the gutter – the inner margin, where the pages are bound together. This will make it hard to read. On the other hand, if your margins are too wide the reading experience will be equally poor because of the large amount of white space around the text. Once again, consistency is the key. Similarly, the space between lines should be enough to make the text readable and legible (i.e. the reader can tell the difference between similar letters such as Q and O). Too narrow a line space will make your text impossible to read. So, in its own way, will too wide a line space.

With a desktop publishing package, you will be able to set up a "style" for your book. The style will include your choice of font, margins, line spacing, heading styles, and chapter heading styles. Simply creating then applying the style up will typeset most of your book. In most cases transferring the text will be a simple copy-and-paste exercise – use the "Control-A" command to select all of the text within your word processor file, use "Control-C" command to copy, then place your cursor at the start of your DTP file and use "Control-V" command to paste. You will most probably need to add additional pages and linked text boxes in order to fit all of your text. However, once this is done, you can use the "Control-A" command to select all of your text, and then apply the style that you have set up for your book.

It is at this point that you need to think about images or diagrams that you need to insert to illustrate your book. There is no point prior to this stage in inserting images into the text, as each edit and change of style will inevitably move the layout of the book. So while it is useful to save your images so that you have them to hand, it is only at the point where you are happy with the final text that you should insert images into the document.

In most cases your images should appear at a resolution of at least 300 dots per inch (dpi). Certainly anything less than 200 (dpi) will appear blurred, "pixelated" or "blocky". Another good reason for using DTP software is that you can set your image sizes using an image "placeholder". This is essentially an image box that can be inserted into the body of your book so that your text wraps around it. You can then insert your chosen image into the box, and the software will automatically size your image to the size of the box. If you are trying to do the same thing in a word processor document, you could only insert the image and try to resize it while simultaneously avoiding the text jumping around it.

It goes without saying that you should be careful about where you source images for your book. You should avoid using other people's images without their permission. This is not simply a matter of courtesy, but a sensible legal precaution. If your book were to turn out to be a bestseller, it would be an expensive shame to find yourself being sued for breach of copyright solely because you copied somebody else's work without permission. The alternatives are creating your own image, searching for open source images, or purchasing a stock image from a platform such as *I-Stock* or *Fotolia*.

The last things to check are "widows" and "orphans". Widows are lines of text that flow over onto a new page.

These are unsightly, and make for difficult reading, especially when they flow from an odd numbered page onto the even-numbered page behind it. Orphans are single words that carry over onto a new page. Clearly, orphans are a greater problem than widows. So while it may be easier to leave a widow than to play around with the layout of the book, you will have to do so to ensure that orphans are brought back onto the same page as the rest of the paragraph they belong to. In most DTP packages you can set up your document for automatic control of widows and orphans. You should also check visually for yourself.

Once all these changes have been made, and you are happy with the look and feel of your book, you need to save it in a format that can be used by the Amazon publishing platforms. While these platforms can manage word processing .doc and .docx files, using these risks messing up your layout in the file conversion process. For this reason saving your work from your DTP package as a .pdf file is preferable, as this should keep all of the formatting in place during the upload and publishing process.

There are several different types of .pdf files. The main difference concerns whether the file is intended to be viewed on a screen or whether it is intended to be printed. This is because a printed document requires different layout and colour profiles to an on-screen document. The main difference being that a screen creates colours from red, green and blue (RGB) primary colours, while print uses cyan, yellow, magenta and black (CYMK) inks to create colours. Fortunately, unless you intend publishing a colour book, you can use a simpler on-screen .pdf file on the CreateSpace platform. The only requirement is that you ensure that you do not place any text or images inside a "safe space" of about 7mm from the edge of the page – if you have set reasonable margins for your page layout, this should not be an issue.

Proof Reading

Proof Reading

You are now ready to "proof read" your final document.

The term "proof reading" comes from a time when setting up a printing press was labour-intensive and expensive. It was only economical to print books in large quantities. So any mistakes would appear in thousands of copies of a book. It has always been essential to check that the printers have typeset the book properly before going to print. To check for any last minute errors, the printer would create an initial proof copy of each of the pages for a publisher to approve prior to printing.

Because it is possible to publish books both electronically and as print-on-demand paperbacks, there is no need to set up an expensive printing press. But this does not mean that you do not need to proof read your final document. Today, most commercial printers will create an electronic .pdf proof for your approval. The extra cost of a printed proof would only be worthwhile if you were planning to print a large number of books. And although you can make bulk orders through CreateSpace, the aim is to take advantage of the print-on-demand system.

The CreateSpace platform includes an online book previewer that shows you how your book will appear in print. It will also flag up obvious errors such as spelling mistakes, problems with images, and any text or objects that run into the "safe zones" at the margins of a page. Here is a screenshot of one of my books at the proof reading stage:

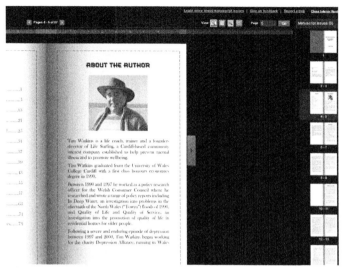

The online previewer is all you need to carry out your final proof reading. CreateSpace also provides a .pdf proof to download and view on screen or print on your home printer.

It is vital that you check thoroughly before approving your files for print. Reviews and ratings are the means by which books are promoted towards the first page of any search on Amazon; so any bad reviews will cost you dearly. While readers will excuse minor typographic errors, they will dislike poor layout. Although it is irritating when you have to go back and alter what you thought was going to be your final .pdf file in order to make the final print version exactly as you wanted it, the effort is worth it in the end. In fact, it is a huge benefit of the CreateSpace system that you are able to make changes by simply amending and reloading your book file until you are happy with it.

Final Details

Final Details

There are a few details to add to your final proof before you publish your book. These come at the beginning of a book, but can only be added when you are ready to publish.

You will need a title page, which gives the reader the full title of your book, the subtitle and the author. On the rear (*verso*) of this page will be your copyright information together with the year your book is published. This page will also include the book's unique International Standard Book Number (ISBN).

Although there is no legal requirement for a book to have an ISBN, it is a useful way of getting your book included in catalogues sent to bookshops and libraries. It is also an Amazon requirement. If you have a publisher, they will assign an ISBN to your book. If you do not, CreateSpace will assign an ISBN for you. You will not be able to do this until you have enrolled your book on the CreateSpace platform. So you will need to copy the two versions (ISBN 10 and ISBN 13) that are assigned to your book, and add them to your Title Verso page.

It is customary to add any dedication you want to make in your book. For example, you might want to thank anyone who has helped with the research, writing, editing or publishing. Alternatively, some people will dedicate a book to a loved one.

If your book deals with professional matters such as law or medicine, or related topics such as dieting or exercising, you may want to add a disclaimer. This will set out the limits of your expertise and will usually advise readers to seek professional advice before relying on anything within the book.

You may want a biography, giving your readers some information about you that is also relevant to the book. You do not have to do this, but if it is relevant it can add authority to your book. For example, in my books about charity, I add information about the 15 years I spent running a charity; in my fundraising book I point out that I have raised more than £650,000 for various causes.

You will need to include a table of contents. This can only be done once you have your final proof, so that you can be sure of the page each chapter starts on. My personal preference is to begin each new chapter on an odd numbered (*recto*) page.

There are also a few things that go at the end of a book. Depending on the nature of your book, you may want to add appendices, an index and bibliography at the end. These are generally only included in academic works. However, they can help readers find source references that you have used in the book.

Finally, if you have published more than one book, you may want to add a page listing your other titles.

Creating Your Book Cover

Creating Your Book Cover

While you may agree with the saying that "you shouldn't judge a book by its cover", the fact is that people do; quite literally so. An attractive cover will draw a reader in to the point that they want to read the opening of your book. So when it comes to selling your book, a great cover design is essential. When your book appears on someone's Amazon search, you need it to look relevant to the subject and professionally designed. Unless your cover grabs a potential reader's attention, they will quickly scroll past it and you will have lost a sale.

Professional design services can be expensive and may be out of the range of a new author. But they can be a useful investment. A professional designer will work up your ideas and add some of his/her own.

You should invest time and effort in making sure you get a cover that sells. This means a cover design that is relevant to the content of the book. It also means ensuring that the cover text stands out and grabs the readers' attention. In part it means getting the overall look and feel of the cover in balance.

It is worth spending time looking at other book covers – particularly those on the same topic as your book – to get ideas about what works and what does not.

There are, broadly, three ways in which you can create a cover for your book for yourself:

- o Use the Amazon cover creator
- o Design a cover as an image

○ Design a cover as a print-ready .pdf file.

The Amazon cover creator is available on both the CreateSpace and Kindle publishing platforms. The cover creator allows you to choose from around 25 cover layouts, each of which can be customised using a wide (but limited) choice of colours and fonts. Each cover can be further customised using any one of more than 900 royalty-free images available within the cover creator. Alternatively, you can upload an image of your own.

The advantage of the cover creator is that it allows you to quickly create a professional looking cover for your book without the need for the particular graphic design skills usually employed to design a book cover. The downside is that your choices of fonts and colours are limited, and your use of stock images may result in your book looking very similar to someone else's.

Among the cover creator templates is one that is empty except for a bleed area and a white space where CreateSpace will impose a barcode that it will generate from your ISBN number. Choosing this option allows you to upload your own cover design as a high-resolution .jpg image file.

There are several types of software that can be used to create an image of your book cover. You could use dedicated graphics software such as Serif's *DrawPlus*, or you could use photograph editing software such as Adobe *Photoshop* or the open source *GIMP* software.

The Ash 5 x 8 Spineless   The Aspen 5 x 8 Spineless   The Birch 5 x 8 Spineless

The Bonsai 5 x 8 Spineless   The Boxelder 5 x 8 Spineless   The Cedar 5 x 8 Spineless

◀ Previous Page   **Page 1 of 5**   Next Page ▶

Some of Amazon's Cover Creator templates

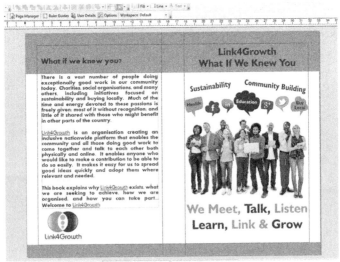

A cover designed in Serif's *PagePlus*

You can create a cover design using the desk top publishing software that you used to produce the final version of your text. The only difference is that you will need to export your cover as an image rather than saving it as a .pdf file.

Creating Your e-book

Creating Your e-book

The final stage in the publishing process is to create the e-book version of your book.

CreateSpace will convert your final print .pdf file into a Kindle (.mobi) file. However, the risk is the same as the risk in trying to convert a word processed document: that the various hidden print commands within the document will conflict with the reading software used by Kindle- and other e-book-readers. This may result in fonts and page layouts suddenly changing halfway through a chapter or even a paragraph, making your e-book appear poorly designed. Bad reviews and low star ratings will follow, guaranteeing that your book will stay at the bottom of people's Amazon searches.

Unfortunately there is no easy way around this. Because each Kindle user is able to set their Kindle device to display according to their own preferences, the only way to guarantee that your book will appear correctly is to create a new version of the book using HTML and CSS* (in the same way as a web designer would if they were creating a web page). Most writers balk at this. After all, they are in the business of writing books not learning to become web designers. But, the process is nowhere near as hard as building a website.

If you really do not feel up to coding your e-book, you might want a company - like Waye Forward (publishing) Ltd - to do this work for you. However, you may relish the challenge of learning to do this for yourself.

---

* Hyper-text mark up language and cascading style sheets are at the core of web design, and are used in the construction of e-books.

The first step is to get rid of all the word processing display commands that exist in the background of your print text file. The easiest way of doing this is to copy the entire body of the text and paste it into the *Notepad* program that comes free with all Windows operating systems. Although this little program makes a fairly lousy word processor, it is actually a very useful (albeit basic) HTML editor.

When you copy your text into *Notepad*, the first thing you will notice is that all the word wrapping has disappeared and each of your paragraphs now appears as a single (very long) line of text. This is because the background styling has been stripped out.

You should now save your file as an .html file. You do this using the drop-down menu that is defaulted to save your file as a .txt file. You should also change the default encoding from "ANSI" to "UTF-8". Once you have done this, if you go to the folder where the file is saved, and click on the file it will open using your default browser.

At this point, you could simply add your HTML and CSS tags to the text within *Notepad*. However, this extremely repetitive and time consuming. My own preference is to use some prototype Adobe software called *Brackets*. This is free coding software that operates in conjunction with Google's *Chrome* browser so that you can see how your e-book looks as you go along.

Here is the opening information for one of my books in *Notepad*:

```
Good Stress - Notepad

File  Edit  Format  View  Help

<P class=booktitle>
Good Stress Bad Stress
</p>

<p class = subtitle>
Rethinking Stress Management</p>

<p class = center>Tim Watkins</p>

<p>
Copyright A© <a href=http://publishing.wayeforwa
</p>

<p>All rights reserved. No part of this publicat

<p class = center>*****</p>

<P class = chapter>ABOUT THE AUTHOR</p>
<p class=center><img src="/wonko1.jpg" alt="Auth

<p>Tim Watkins is a life coach, trainer and a fo
<p>Tim Watkins graduated from the University of
<p>Between 1990 and 1997 he worked as a policy r
</p>
<p>Following a severe and enduring episode of de
</p>
<p>In October 2010, along with Julia Kaye and Pa
</p>
<p class = center>*****</p>

<P class = chapter>INTRODUCTION</p>

<p>We have been taught to view stress as an illr
</p>
<p>From this perspective, stress is an enemy to
</p>
<p>But how do we square this desire to avoid or
</p>
<p>One answer to these questions is that our bel
</p>
<p>A second answer is that our view of successfu
</p>
```

Here is the same information transferred into *Brackets*:

```
106   <P class=booktitle>
107   Good Stress Bad Stress
108   </p>
109
110   <p class = subtitle>
111   Rethinking Stress Management</p>
112
113   <p class = center>Tim Watkins</p>
114
115   <p>
116   Copyright © <a href=http://publishing.waye
117   </p>
118
119   <p>All rights reserved. No part of this pu
      system, or transmitted, in any form or by
      recording or otherwise, without the prior
120
121   <p class = center>*****</p>
122
123   <P class = chapter>ABOUT THE AUTHOR</p>
124   <p class=center><img src="/Wonkol.jpg" alt
125
126   <p>Tim Watkins is a life coach, trainer an
      surfing.com/>Life Surfing</a>, a Cardiff-b
      prevent mental illness and to promote well
127   <p>Tim Watkins graduated from the Universi
      economics degree in 1990.</p>
128   <p>Between 1990 and 1997 he worked as a po
      where he researched and wrote a range of p
      into problems in the aftermath of the Nort
      and Quality of Service, an investigation i
      homes for older people.
129   </p>
```

And this is how it displays in the *chrome* browser – an approximation of how it will display on a Kindle device:

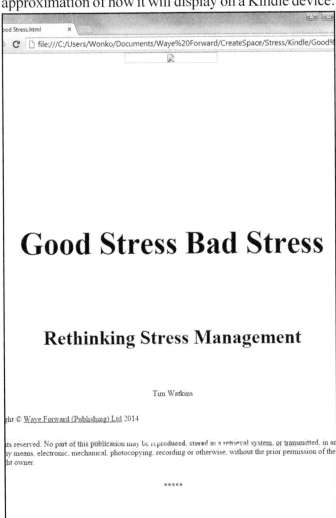

Websites (and e-books) have a structure – chapters, sections, paragraphs, etc – and a style – fonts, type sizes, line heights, paragraph indents, etc. HTML (hyper-text mark-up language) is used to create the structure. CSS (cascading style sheets) is used to determine the style.

Most websites keep structure and styling in different files. But in an e-book they must all be contained in a single file. So an e-book file will be separated into three distinct parts:

○ The file type

○ The head (which contains the styling – CSS – code)

○ The body (which contains the structure – HTML – code).

The file type information tells a browser or an e-book reader what type of file this is:

```
<?xml version="1.0" encoding="utf-8"?>

<!DOCTYPE html PUBLIC "-//W3C//DTD XHTML 1.0 Strict//EN"

"http://www.w3.org/TR/xhtml1/DTD/xhtml1-strict.dtd">
```

Without this code at the beginning of your e-book file, the e-book reader will be unable to decipher the content of the file.

The next section of your e-book file is called the "Head" which is signalled to the e-book reader with the tags: <head></head>. These act like a container, telling the e-book reader that everything between them is part of the Head. Indeed, anything relating to the HTML structure of the file opens with a <...> tag and closes with a <.../> tag. For example, a paragraph would begin <p> and close with </p>. In an e-book the Head will contain all of the styling codes:

```
<style type="text/css"></style>
```

So an e-book device can see that everything written between the two tags is about how the remainder of the contents is to be displayed.

In order to prevent any styles conflicting with those already pre-set by your readers in their Kindle devices, you need to begin by setting all styles in your book to zero. To do this you insert this line of code:

```
html, body, div, h1, h2, h3, h4, h5, h6, ul, ol, dl, li, dt, dd, p,
pre, table, th, td, tr { margin: 0; padding: 0em; }
```

You are then ready to insert the styles that you need for your book to display as you want it.

The CSS code that I use to style a paragraph is written like this:

```
p
   {
     text-indent: 0em;
     margin-bottom: 2em;
   }
```

(It is customary to indent each line of code to make it easier to read). The letter "p" tells the e-book device that every time it encounters the HTML code <p> for "paragraph" it should apply the style set out between the {...} brackets. So, I have chosen just two styles for my basic paragraphs; that the text should not be indented but that after each paragraph there should be a bottom margin that is two times the size of the letter "m" (2em). The letter "m" is used because it is square (i.e. the same width and height). Done in this way, it means that irrespective of the font and font size set up on someone's Kindle device, there will always be a space equivalent to two letter "m"s after a paragraph.

While adding spaces between paragraphs is the convention for non-fiction, paragraphs in works of fiction generally follow on the next line, but start with an indent. To achieve this, we simple reverse the code:

```
p
 {
   text-indent: 2em;
   margin-bottom: 0em;
 }
```

You will need to create distinct styles for each of the different types of text that appear within your book. For example, your title text needs to be different from a subtitle, and both need to be different from a chapter heading. All three must stand out from ordinary paragraphs. Here is the code I use for book titles:

```
p.booktitle
{
        margin-top:5em;
        margin-bottom:2em;
        text-indent: 0em;
        text-align:center;
```

```
    font-weight: bold;
    font-size: 4em;
}
```

This sets margins of 5 letter "m"s above and 2 "m"s below my title text. The text is centred, bold and 4 "m"s in height.

When I code the title text in my book I use the code:

```
<p class=booktitle>Title Text</p>
```

A kindle device (or web browser) will see the "p class" element and know that it is not dealing with a standard paragraph. It will look for the styling that corresponds to the "p class=booktitle" and will find it in the "p.booktitle" styling.

Similarly, my subtitle is coded:

```
p.subtitle
    {
        margin-top:2em;
        margin-bottom:2em;
        text-indent: 0 em;
        text-align:center;
        font-weight: bold;
        font-size: 2.5em;
        page-break-after: always;
    }
```

So my subtitle text can then be coded:

```
<p class=subtitle>Subtitle text</p>
```

Again, the Kindle device knows to look for the style for a subtitle.

I strongly recommend using the W3Schools (www.w3schools.com) website to learn more about coding, and to copy and paste any lines of code that you require for your e-book. After all, it is your book, so you should design it to your preferences, not mine.

The third (final) part of your e-book file is the "body" or structure of your book. This is coded using the tags: <body></body>. This tells the e-reader that everything between these two switches is included in the structure of the document.

Most of what appears in the body of the file will be plain old paragraphs <p></p>. The most tedious part of preparing an e-book version of your work will be the process of going through your document adding these tags at the start and end of each paragraph.

There are other structures within the text. For example, we have looked at book titles and a subtitle. In a recent book that I published I had to create 10 different styles:

1. The book title
2. The subtitle
3. Chapter headings
4. Text headings
5. Paragraphs
6. Indented paragraphs
7. Lists

8.Quotes

9.Centred text

10.Endnotes.

Each of these required different styles, but each used the basic paragraph style as a starting point. So the code for each started "p." For example, the CSS code I use for a quote is:

```
p.quote
    {
            margin-top: 2em;
            margin-right: 2em;
            margin-bottom:2em;
            margin-left: 2em;
    }
```

This CSS code in the Head of the document corresponds to the HTML tags: <p class=quote></p> in the Body. So each time the Kindle device finds this HTML code, it knows to display it in the style set out in the corresponding CSS code. So, in the style I created, Kindle device would know that it should insert a margin that is two times the size of the letter "m" on all sides of the text.

Some styling can be added directly within the HTML code. For example the code: <strong></strong> is the HTML equivalent of the bold button (or "control b") in your word processor, telling the Kindle device that everything that appears between the two tags should be displayed in bold. Similarly, the code <em></em> is the equivalent to the italics button (or "control i") in your word processor.

Using the Adobe *Brackets* software (see tools of the trade) you can build the styles you require, and then test them to see how they will look using the Google *Chrome* browser. When you modify a style, then save it, it will automatically update the display in *Chrome*. In this way, you can experiment with alignment and sizing to give the book the look and feel that you want.

Most of your document can be coded using either the paragraph code <p>… </p> or a paragraph class <p class=…>…</p>, but there are some elements that require an additional type of code using the tags: <a></a>. The three of these that you are most likely to require in an e-book are:

○ Images

○ Endnotes[*]

○ Links.

The HTML code for an Image is:

```
<img src="url" alt="some descriptive text">
```

The "url" element refers to the place where the Kindle device can find the image file. Since, when you come to package your e-book, your HTML file and any images that you want within the book will all be in the same folder, all you need insert is a forward slash "/"

---

[*] Unlike a printed book, an e-book does not have pages but is essentially a continuous document; there is no way to ensure footnotes appear at the bottom of the correct page.

together with the full name and type of the image (e.g. "/image.jpg"). The "alt" element refers to the alternative text that should display in the event of the image not displaying properly. In most cases this will be a brief description of the image. It is important to include the "alt" element and text, as without it the Kindle device will not be able to display the image.

The code for a Link is

```
<a href="url">the link text</a>
```

Here, the "url" element is the web address that you are referring to. The "the link text" element is the text that you wish to display in your e-book. This is especially important where the Internet page you are linking to has a very long address, as it allows you to create the link without having to display it.

Endnotes are trickier to code because they require three elements:

○ A reference point within your text (usually a number)

○ The corresponding endnote

○ A "back" button to return the reader to the reference point in the text.

The code for a reference point in the text is:

```
<a href="#en1">[1]</a>
```

The number (1 in this case) corresponds to the number of the endnote.

Although the endnote itself could use the code:

```
<p><a name="fn1">[1]</a> endnote text</p>
```

(The "endnote text" is the body of the note) this would not enable readers to get back to their starting point in the main text. To achieve this you need to use the code:

```
<a id="footNote1">  <sup>[1]</sup></a>
<pclass="endnote-text">endnote text here(<a href="#BkMkToFoot1">Go Back</a>)</p>
```

In this case, the "Go Back" text will appear in brackets at the end of the note and will provide a link back to the reference point within the main text.

The tags are used so that the endnote number appears in superscript (like this: [1])

This is all the basic coding that you are likely to need to know in order to create your e-book. But this is not the place to attempt to teach you how to fully code either a website or an e-book in full. You can use the www.w3schools.com website to learn more about HTML and CSS coding for yourself.

Once you have gone through your text, coding the structure and styling that you require, and viewed this in your Google *Chrome* browser, you will be able to save a final .html file. This should be saved in a folder that also contains any images contained in your book. I generally set up a single folder for each e-book I publish. This contains the raw text (from *Notepad*) the HTML file (from *Brackets*) together with copies of any images I want within the book.

The next step is to convert your e-book folder into a final e-book file that can be read by an e-reader. To do this we need a piece of software called *Calibre 64 bit*.

This is a free open source package that was created to convert .html files into several different types of e-book files.

You will first need to "compress" the folder containing the file and any images contained in the book into a new .zip folder. You can do this simply by right clicking the folder and selecting "zip". You can then load this compressed folder into *Calibre 64 bit*. You will then be prompted to enter your book's metadata (i.e. the name of the author, title of the book, publisher and search keywords). *Calibre 64 bit* will also generate a table of contents and add your cover image for your e-book.

Once you have completed this process, you are ready to convert your book into a .mobi file that can be uploaded to the Amazon Kindle platform for publication. *Calibre 64 bit* automatically creates your .mobi file and shows you a preview of how the book will look on a Kindle reader. However, on occasion the preview within *Calibre 64 bit* will be different to the way your book will display on a Kindle device. For this reason, you may wish to download the free Kindle preview app from the Amazon Kindle website.

You should preview your e-book thoroughly (in the same way as you previewed and proof read your print-ready .pdf file before you uploaded it for printing). Only when you are happy with the way your book displays on Kindle preview should you begin to upload it to the Kindle platform.

The Amazon Publishing Platforms

The Amazon Publishing Platforms

At this point, you have created two final versions of your book:

○ A print-ready .pdf file that you will use for the paperback version of your book (you may also use this as a stand-alone e-book for download from your website), and

○ A Kindle .mobi file that you will use as your Kindle book.

The next step is to upload each of these files to its respective Amazon platforms.

The platform for creating print-on-demand paperback books is called CreateSpace[*]. You will need to create a new (free) account to get started. Once you have done this, you can follow the step-by-step instructions for creating your book.

One final editorial change to your final .pdf file is the addition of two ISBN codes (ISBN 10 and ISBN 13) that CreateSpace will generate and assign to your book. These numbers will be inserted into the bibliographical information page at the beginning of your book - this page usually includes details of the publisher together with a copyright notice. You will also need to leave a blank space on the rear cover of your book so that CreateSpace can include your ISBN in numeric and barcode formats for the book to sell on the Amazon website and in official book publishers' catalogues.

Alternatively, you can purchase and use your own

---

[*] www.createspace.com

ISBN number. However, a block of 10 ISBN numbers will cost you £132 (as of December 2014), so this is only worth doing if you intend publishing several books. If you are using your own ISBN, you will still need to use the CreateSpace platform to generate the ISBN 10 number.

You can follow the step-by-step CreateSpace process to input your book's details (title, subtitle, author's details, etc). You will then be prompted to select and upload the print-ready .pdf file of your book.

Once the upload is complete, you will be prompted to review your book in a preview window. This will allow you to see any errors, and to check that the file has uploaded properly. If it has not, you can go back and change the file as many times as you need to get it right. Once you are happy with the preview, you can approve it for publication.

The Kindle platform* process is very similar, although there is no requirement for an ISBN number (you cannot use the same number as the print version as this is treated separately to the e-book version). You will be prompted to enter your book's details then asked to select and upload your file. You will then be asked to preview your book using an online version of the free Kindle reading app. The difference between the Kindle and print review windows is that the Kindle review window allows you to check how your book will appear in a range of different Kindle devices.

---

* www.kdp.amazon.com

On both platforms, once you have uploaded and approved your book, you will be invited to choose a cover design. You are offered three choices:

- Upload your cover as a .pdf file
- Choose an Amazon design and cover image using their cover creator online software
- Use a cover creator template to create your own cover image.

If you have already created a cover design of your own, and have saved it as a .pdf file, you will be able to upload it directly. The CreateSpace design team will review your file and either make minor alterations that are required, or suggest changes. Once you are happy with the final version, you will need to approve it for print.

If you decide to use the cover creator platform, you will be guided, step by step through a choice of 30 templates, each of which includes five or six styles. You will be able to choose the colour of your book cover, and you can use one of more than 900 royalty-free images.

Within the cover creator platform is an option to upload your cover design as an image. You can select a template, which shows you the areas where you can add text and images. This also includes the blank space for your barcode ISBN. You simply upload your cover design as an image, and let CreateSpace process it.

You will be invited to review your final cover. Again, you can go back and amend and resubmit your cover as many times as it takes to get it right.

Once you have approved content and cover design, you will be invited to set prices for your book and e-book, and to register the bank account into which your royalties should be paid. There are no hard and fast rules about pricing your paperback book. The only requirement is that your books sell for more than they cost to print. You will then receive a 70 percent royalty (minus the print cost) on every book you sell. A sensible approach is to search for the prices of similar books. You should set a similar price rather than undercut them by charging too little. A low price will make your book look inferior.

The Kindle platform is different. You can only receive the 70 percent royalty rate if you agree to sell your book exclusively on Kindle. In practice, this is no hardship as, at present, none of the other e-book platforms is popular enough to provide more than token royalties. In order to obtain the 70 percent royalty rate, you will also have to agree to keep the price of your Kindle book within a price band set by Amazon - currently between $2.99 (£1.80) and $9.99 (£6.02)*. Again, this is not a hardship, as there are no print setup costs with e-books. Too high a price will deter potential readers.

The Kindle platform also offers a "Kindle Select" programme. If you enrol your book in this programme,

---

* Recently, Amazon has been testing pricing software that shows you the optimal price for Kindle e-books similar to yours.

Amazon Prime customers will be able to borrow your book. And each time a book is borrowed – and more than 10 percent of the content is read – you will receive a payment (which is often greater than the royalty you receive when you sell a book). The other benefit of enrolling in Kindle Select is that it enables you to run promotions on your book. You can either run:

○ A "countdown promotion" in which the price of your book is reduced for a period of up to a week

○ A free offer on your book for up to a week.

Why would you want to do this?

The benefits of these offers are to do with the way books sell on Amazon. Unless you are very good (or very lucky) you are not going to end up on the first page of anyone's search for a title on Amazon. But have you noticed that when you look at an item on Amazon, you are presented with a row of additional products under the banner "customers who viewed this also bought this"? This is why cut-price and free offers are important - they count as sales. So the more people downloading your book, the more likely it will appear next to other books that they have bought, thereby making your book more visible.

Reviews and ratings are the other big promotional currency on the Amazon website. Books with lots of 5-star ratings will appear highly on searches ordered according to popularity. Also, Amazon gives more weight to books that receive positive reviews. So, again, by occasionally giving books away or selling them at low cost, you are increasing your reviews and ratings.

A final consideration with the CreateSpace and Kindle platforms concerns the USA/UK tax treaties. Both set up their users' self-publishing accounts in the USA for tax purposes. Because of this their systems have a default to withhold 30 percent of your royalties as a USA sales tax. However, since UK individuals and companies are covered by a tax treaty, you are not legally required to pay US taxes on your royalties (although you will have to include them in your UK tax return, and may have to pay income tax on them here). Both platforms provide the necessary tax declaration forms for you to complete. However, you will need to make a telephone call to the US Internal Revenue Service to obtain a tax identification number and a certificate that exempts you from US taxes.

This can be a bureaucratic and time consuming process. It is another reason to consider working with a self-publishing company.

Marketing

Marketing

When you self-publish a book on Amazon, it automatically appears on the Amazon website. But this does not guarantee sales. And while Amazon has an interest in selling your book, they will give it no more attention than they give to the millions of other titles. Getting sales is down to you!

In the end, the amount of sales you generate will be down to two factors:

1. The market for your book
2. The amount of work you are prepared to put into selling it.

Your "market" is the number of people interested in the subject of your book multiplied by the amount they are prepared to pay to read it. A very small niche market could be lucrative if the people within it are prepared to pay a high price for books on this topic. On the other hand, a large market may not be that lucrative if buyers are not prepared to pay for additional books on that topic. If your book is aimed at a wider mass market, you may have to sell it for a much lower price.

Because you are dealing with a global market when you publish on Amazon, it may be difficult to calculate the size of the market. However, you can look at similar books to get an idea of how popular they are and the price they sell for. Amazon provides a sales ranking as well as the price of all books on its website.

When you search for a book on any topic, Amazon will display the results so that those with lots of good ratings and reviews appear first. Unfortunately, Amazon frown on authors soliciting reviews for their books, and they will penalise you if you get caught doing it. However, there are many things that you can do to encourage people to buy your book - both online and offline. If you do not have a blog, sign up for one. If you intend publishing several books, you may want to invest in your own website. You can get a free Google blog. You can then create short articles related to your book, and add links to your book for readers of your blog to follow. If you have a website or a blog, you could make the first chapter of your book available to readers. If it is well written, and captures your readers' attention, they will most likely buy a copy.

You should also create social media accounts on Google+, Facebook and Twitter. These can be used to post comments related to your book. Indeed, most successful authors begin a social media dialogue with potential readers many months before their book is published.

If you are certain that your book is going to sell, you might consider online advertising. Google ads and Facebook ads operate on a pay-per-click basis, in which you only pay if someone clicks on the link in your advert. This can be very risky with book sales because the cost of advertising will quickly exceed your royalties unless the majority of those who click through to your book actually buy it.

Although your book will be sold online, remember to market it off line. Most obviously, arrange to give talks on the subject of your book. You can either set up a talk yourself, or you could make yourself available to book clubs and social groups - particularly those with an interest in its subject. If your book is on a newsworthy topic, you could put out a press release to media organisations that might be interested in it. If your book is on a niche topic, it is well worth researching titles and programmes that cover the topic.

You might also want to visit local bookshops to see whether they will stock your books, perhaps on a sale or return basis - you might even be able to arrange a book signing event that will both publicise your book and their bookshop.

Good Luck

Good Luck

In this book I have set out the steps involved in creating your book, from getting your initial thoughts down on (electronic) paper through to publishing your book and beginning to earn royalties from it.

The number of books you sell and the amount of income you earn from your book will, in large part, depend on the amount of effort you are prepared to put into promoting it both online (using blogs, social media and advertising) and offline (using press-releases, talks and book signings).

You may decide that you do not want to learn all of the elements of book publishing or that creating your e-book is too demanding. Or you may need some additional coaching and mentoring. In this case, I hope that you contact me or my colleagues at Waye Forward (Publishing) Ltd to find out more about how we can help you to publish your book.

Finally, I wish you well with your book, and may it add to the knowledge and richness of humanity.

Tim Watkins, January 2015.

Appendix - Software

Appendix - Software

I have referred to twenty-four software packages that are necessary to writing, editing, typesetting, designing and publishing your book. Here is a list of these packages together with the Internet links to the sites where you can obtain them:

Open Source (free) Software

Adobe Brackets:

http://brackets.io

Calibre 64 Bit:

http://calibre-ebook.com/download_windows64

GIMP:

http://www.gimp.org

Google Chrome:

www.google.com/chrome

Google Docs:

www.google.co.uk/docs/about

Kindle Previewer:

http://www.amazon.com/gp/feature.html?docId=10007
65261

KindleGen:

http://www.amazon.com/gp/feature.html?docId
=1000765211

Open Office:

www.openoffice.org

ProWritingAid:

https://prowritingaid.com

Scribus:

www.scribus.net

It is entirely possible to create and publish your book solely using this open source software. This said, the commercial software packages that I refer to in the book are more versatile and often much easier to work with. Much will depend on your time and budget.

Commercial Software

Adobe Creative Suite:

http://www.adobe.com/uk/creativecloud.html

Adobe InDesign:

www.adobe.com/uk/products/indesign.html

Adobe Photoshop:

http://www.adobe.com/uk/products/photoshop.html

Auto Crit:

www.autocrit.com

Dragon Naturally Speaking:

http://www.nuance.co.uk/dragon

MS Office:

https://office.live.com

MS Publisher:

https://products.office.com/en-us/publisher

MS Word:

http://products.office.com/en-us/word

MS WordPad:

http://windows.microsoft.com/en-GB/ windows7/
products/features/wordpad

Scrivener:

http://www.literatureandlatte.com/scrivener.php

Serif DrawPlus:

www.serif.com/drawplus

Serif PagePlus:

www.serif.com/pageplus

Serif PhotoPlus:

www.serif.com/photoplus

Zotero:

www.zotero.org

About Waye Forward

Waye Forward has published a range of books - both clients' books and our own. Now we would like to help you to publish your book too.

We provide a complete package of support:

○ Coaching and mentoring
○ Editing and proof reading
○ Typesetting and cover design
○ Publishing

Whether you are just beginning to think about writing a book, or have a finished work that you are happy with, why not let us help you get the best from your work?

publishing.wayeforward.com

Also By Tim Watkins

- *Beating Anxiety: A Guide to Managing and Overcoming Anxiety Disorders.*

- *Depression: A guide to managing and overcoming depression.*

- *Depression Workbook: 70 Self-help techniques for recovering from depression.*

- *Distress to De-stress: Understanding and managing stress in everyday life.*

- *Food for Mood: A guide to healthy eating for mental health. for anyone who is relatively new to cooking.*

- *Getting to sleep: A guide to overcoming stress-related sleep problem.*

- *Good Stress - Bad Stress: Rethinking stress management.*

- *How to Help: A guide to helping someone manage mental distress.*

- *Helping Hands: How to Help Someone Else Cope with Mental Health Problems.*

- *No More Panic - A Guide to overcoming panic attacks and recovering from panic disorder.*

- *Smart Fundraising: A guide to fundraising for small charities and community groups.*

Printed in Great Britain
by Amazon